CAMBRIDGE LIBRARY COLLECTION

Books of enduring scholarly value

Cambridge

The city of Cambridge received its royal charter in 1201, having already been home to Britons, Romans and Anglo-Saxons for many centuries. Cambridge University was founded soon afterwards and celebrates its octocentenary in 2009. This series explores the history and influence of Cambridge as a centre of science, learning, and discovery, its contributions to national and global politics and culture, and its inevitable controversies and scandals.

Cambridge and Charles Lamb

Although the early nineteenth-century essayist Charles Lamb never studied in Cambridge, he knew the city well and had many friends connected with the University, most notably Samuel Taylor Coleridge. Between 1909 and 1914, at a time when Lamb was widely read and admired, a series of dinners were held in Cambridge to commemorate Lamb's birthday and his connections with the city. Edited by one of the original organisers, George Wherry, in 1925, this little volume collects his reminiscences of eminent guests at the events, along with two informative essays on Lamb's Cambridge connections by Lamb's biographer and editor E. V. Lucas. Another contribution is Edmund Gosse's account of how his friendship with Algernon Swinburne was enriched by their shared admiration of Lamb. The volume remains of interest both as a record of Edwardian academic conviviality, remembered after the Great War, and of the enthusiasm Lamb inspired at the time.

Cambridge University Press has long been a pioneer in the reissuing of out-of-print titles from its own backlist, producing digital reprints of books that are still sought after by scholars and students but could not be reprinted economically using traditional technology. The Cambridge Library Collection extends this activity to a wider range of books which are still of importance to researchers and professionals, either for the source material they contain, or as landmarks in the history of their academic discipline.

Drawing from the world-renowned collections in the Cambridge University Library, and guided by the advice of experts in each subject area, Cambridge University Press is using state-of-the-art scanning machines in its own Printing House to capture the content of each book selected for inclusion. The files are processed to give a consistently clear, crisp image, and the books finished to the high quality standard for which the Press is recognised around the world. The latest print-on-demand technology ensures that the books will remain available indefinitely, and that orders for single or multiple copies can quickly be supplied.

The Cambridge Library Collection will bring back to life books of enduring scholarly value across a wide range of disciplines in the humanities and social sciences and in science and technology.

Cambridge and Charles Lamb

George Edward Wherry

CAMBRIDGE UNIVERSITY PRESS

Cambridge New York Melbourne Madrid Cape Town Singapore São Paolo Delhi

Published in the United States of America by Cambridge University Press, New York

www.cambridge.org
Information on this title: www.cambridge.org/9781108002547

© in this compilation Cambridge University Press 2009

This edition first published 1925
This digitally printed version 2009

ISBN 978-1-108-00254-7

CAMBRIDGE
AND
CHARLES LAMB

CAMBRIDGE
UNIVERSITY PRESS
LONDON : Fetter Lane

NEW YORK
The Macmillan Co.
BOMBAY, CALCUTTA AND
MADRAS
Macmillan and Co., Ltd.
TORONTO
The   Macmillan   Co. of
Canada, Ltd.
TOKYO
Maruzen-Kabushiki-Kaisha

CHARLES LAMB
in the dress of a Venetian
Senator

(*From the painting by*
William Hazlitt)

CAMBRIDGE
AND CHARLES LAMB

Edited by

GEORGE WHERRY
M.Chir., F.R.C.S.

_

CAMBRIDGE

AT THE UNIVERSITY PRESS

1925

CONTENTS

ILLUSTRATIONS

I

THE CAMBRIDGE
CHARLES LAMB
DINNERS

by
George Wherry

¶ In Memoriam: Charles Sayle

My pleasant neighbour, gone before
To that unknown and silent shore,
Shall we not meet as heretofore,
Some Summer morning.

IN the founding and organising of the Cambridge Charles Lamb Dinners perhaps the largest part was played by Charles Sayle and it is in memory of him that this account of them has been compiled.

These dinners—six in all—were held in each of the years 1909 to 1914, when the War brought them to an end.

Sayle's life peculiarly fitted him for this agreeable task. Educated at Rugby School and New College, he returned after a brief period in London to his old home at Cambridge, and joined St John's College. He devoted himself to bibliographical work and became an Under-Librarian in the University Library. His knowledge of books enabled him to give valuable help to enquirers in every branch of learning and in the pursuit of references and quotations he spared no pains.

At the Library he came into contact with most of the literary men in the University and thus it was easy for him to collect those who would be likely to sympathise with the idea of a Lamb Dinner.

But it was his great gift of gaining touch with undergraduates which was of most help in drawing to the table the best of the younger men. For many years Sayle had succeeded in gathering undergraduates to his house in Trumpington Street, a bachelor abode, rather hidden back from the main street, small but commodious, with a room upstairs which held an old Broadwood grand piano.

Generations of undergraduates came to his quarters for literary talk, with intervals of music. Since his death long letters have come to me—I hope many came to him in his lifetime—all bearing testimony to the help those evenings gave. Maurice Berkeley, of Pembroke, wrote:

Any ability I have acquired in appreciating music, which previously I could not understand, I owe entirely to Sayle.

Charles E. Lambe wrote from his ship *Benbow*, off Malta:

Sayle's gift of collecting round him a little company of undergraduates was remarkable, if only because youth is not easily attracted by its seniors. I feel he must have done it by some subtle form of flattery, very discreet and very indirect. He made you feel, even on first meeting him, that you were worthy of his attention, which he gave undividedly. When one is young, and I imagine afterwards as well, this is a pleasing factor, and it seems to me that to this special quality Sayle largely owed his popularity with younger men....Sayle was a great listener—with few words he would draw one out in an amazing way.

A. Macdonald, of Repton School, wrote that he treasured "thirty or forty pages of trifling notes" which he "would not exchange for a far more printable correspondence."

"There is," so ran the letter, "a touch of melancholy, but of the best kind, in a sentence in a recent letter, 'My road for the rest of the journey seems mostly downhill.' We watched his descent too calmly, forgetting that the last mile is often so steep, and he disappeared through the haze into the pleasant Inn of Death before we had even time to say Good-bye to him."

Sayle was very fond of flowers, especially white flowers, and sedulously cultivated his garden, hidden away behind the house and guarded by high old walls of dark brick. The little house and garden always reminded me of Herrick's song of "littles," with his maid "Prew," for there was always a Prudence Baldwin to look after Sayle. The garden was used in summer for the Sunday evenings which for years became an important part of his life, "that best portion of a good man's life"—the thousand "little unremembered acts of kindness and of love."

In this house he died in his sixtieth year, having reached the same age as Charles Lamb.

ℂ THE FIRST DINNER

Among Sayle's papers evidence was found by Mr A. T. Bartholomew that he intended to write an account of the Charles Lamb Dinners at some future time, but not a line on the subject was discovered. It was natural that the editor of Sir Thomas Browne should love Charles Lamb and seek to perpetuate his memory. As Ainger has pointed out, Browne was the author most frequently quoted in the *Essays* and *Letters*.

It was an old idea of Sayle's, and as far back as 1905 I find a note:

The Vice-Master of Trinity [Aldis Wright] wants to know if you care to subscribe anything up to half-a-sovereign to a Charles Lamb Tablet to be erected on the house he occupied at Enfield. He got 5s. out of me.

Later, when the gravestone of Charles Isola, on the north side of the church of St Mary the Less, was found to be broken across, we, with the help of Canon Stokes, repaired the stone. This was in memory of the father of Emma

Isola, Lamb's adopted daughter, who married Moxon, the publisher[1].

In 1908 a small society was formed, of which Mr A. T. Bartholomew of the Library, Sayle, and myself were the most active members, and over little dinners at my house we met to discuss the founding of an Annual Dinner in memory of Lamb. Many difficulties had to be overcome, and first, that as Lamb was not a Cambridge man, in the sense of having belonged to a College, there was no obvious place for such a feast. The Pepys dinner was, of course, held at Magdalene College, and a Coleridge dinner (such as was once suggested by Mr Arthur Gray) would naturally have been held at Jesus.

The Samuel Johnson supper, held at Lichfield, seemed the nearest to what we proposed. Being homeless, we decided to dine in the University Arms Hotel; to invite our guests; to have one guest of the evening and to obtain a chairman from the University. As undergraduates were to be asked to join, it was necessary to gain permission, which was duly accorded:

I give permission to Mr C. E. Sayle of St John's College to arrange for a dinner for 70 persons at the University Arms Hotel.

H. F. Stewart, Senior Proctor.

[1] See p. 44.

The date of February 10th was that of Lamb's birthday, but the Saturday nearest the birthday enabled week-end visitors to attend and was therefore chosen. Our project met with much encouragement in the University, and had, moreover, a good send-off in the recent publication of *The Life of Charles and Mary Lamb*, by Mr E. V. Lucas—a book which had reminded many of their old love.

Mr Augustine Birrell was asked to come as our guest, and kindly promised to do so if only his Parliamentary duties permitted—he was at that time Secretary of State for Ireland, and there was some uncertainty about his visit. Acceptances came in very well and indeed more might have been gathered if a dinner of forty guests had not seemed large enough.

In spite of all this support we could not persuade anyone to preside at our feast, and at the last moment I had to take the chair, and as Chairman, it was my duty to introduce Mr Birrell:

"We are here to-night in honour of literature, and to commemorate the birth of Charles Lamb. We meet upon a date near upon his birthday, which was on February the 10th, 1775. It is related of Thackeray that, reading one of Lamb's letters containing a tender passage to a child, and thinking on Lamb's life, he put the letter to his lips and said '*Saint Charles.*' Thackeray was right! With all those who, like ourselves, distinguish *goodness* from goodyness, Charles Lamb *was* a saint. In the Roman Church, I believe, three qualifications are necessary for sainthood: first, that there should be a life which displayed great fortitude and charity; secondly, that the candidate should be worshipped during that life; and thirdly, that miracles should have been wrought after death. Charles Lamb is blessed by us on all these points exactly. He manifested during his life the greatest amount of fortitude and cheerful courage; in his lifetime was adored 'on this side idolatry'; and what miracles have not his 'midnight darlings' wrought, since his death, in many a sad heart!

"He is honoured, though not beneath the dome of St Peter's; but we ourselves are the cardinals who have canonised him in our hearts.

"It is fitting that in Cambridge we should celebrate this event. The old universities held Lamb's deep affection, and especially he loved Cambridge, for Lamb felt strongly the genius of places. It was here that he wrote the essay 'Oxford in the Vacation,' Oxford standing for Cambridge with his usual mystification. Here, at the house of Mrs Paris, he met his adopted child—Emma Isola—daughter of the Esquire

Bedell, and granddaughter of the Cambridge
teacher who taught Italian to Wordsworth.

"Lamb's interest contained a strange assortment such as Crisp the Barber, Richard Hopkins the swearing scullion, afterwards cook of
Trinity Hall and Caius.

"And Mrs Smith. 'Ask anyone,' he says,
'who is the biggest woman in Cambridge?
They will tell you *Mrs Smith*, who broke down
the bench, between Trinity and St John's, and
was the cause of litigation between the societies
as to who should repair it!' She became the
gentle giantess and widow Blackett of Oxford.
'Oxford,' he says, 'in vacation could never be
said to be empty, having *thee* to fill it.'

"Lamb notes the college cat, and the college
portraits. He approves them all.

"And then his best friends were Cambridge
men. Coleridge was at Jesus when Lamb wrote
the 'Monologue to a Young Jackass in Jesus
Piece,' but better than this he spoke of 'the
friendly cloisters and happy groves of quiet
ever-honoured Jesus.' Wordsworth was at St
John's, where he enjoyed to the full 'the ad-
vantages to be derived from the neglect of his
Teachers.' Charles Valentine le Grice, his old
schoolfellow, was at Trinity. Of him Gunning
relates the story of how he shouted a noisy song

on King's Parade as the V.C. was going to
church—with the refrain 'Gadzoons, gadzoons,
Lowther Yates in pantaloons!' and how the
silver-tongued undergraduate soothed the rage
of the V.C. and was forgiven. Charles Lloyd
resided in Cambridge for a time, and did a good
deed in introducing Lamb to Manning.—
Thomas Manning of Gonville and Caius, 'the
friendly, the mathematical Manning.'

"Is there anywhere in literature a more mar-
vellous blending of pathos and humour than in
Lamb's letter beseeching Manning not to go to
China—not to go among the Manchus, people
with a name like that must be *cannibals*—not to
go among 'nasty, unconversable, horse-belching
Tartars.' Well, Manning grew his great beard
and spent his years in China and Thibet, was
the first Englishman in Lhassa, and saw the
grand Llama; a scholar, and a great traveller,
but known to the world as the friend of Lamb.

"One word about George Dyer, of the 'House
of Pure Emmanuel,' Amicus Redivivus, the
G. D. of 'Oxford in the Vacation[1].'

"Dyer was very short-sighted, and walked
in broad daylight straight into the New River,
which was opposite Lamb's house at Islington.
Dyer was on his way to see Mrs Barbauld—you

[1] For a fuller account of Dyer, see pp. 59 ff.

may remember that at that time there was
also a Mrs Inchbald, and Lamb used to call
them the two *bald women*. What delicious fun
was poked at Dyer by Lamb, but with what
wisdom and practical kindness he managed him.
In the Fitzwilliam Museum is a picture of Dyer,
which must have been taken after the widow
married him and washed and brushed him up.

"I have had this portrait photographed as a
souvenir of this dinner, so that it can be placed
in the volume of Essays opposite 'Amicus
Redivivus,' and preserved with Mr Sayle's
literary menu[1].

"Now I turn to another of Lamb's Cambridge
friends, who needs no introduction; who, loving
Lamb himself, has made others love him. We
thank him for coming here to-night, and sparing
a moment from his arduous duties. I ask you
to drink the health of Mr Birrell, the guest of
the evening."

Mr Birrell, in a delightful speech, welcomed
by name some of the guests in a way both
intimate and charming. Unfortunately there is

[1] A detailed account of this portrait and of the
identity of the dog is given by Major Butterworth
in the *Cambridge Review* for 30 May, 1912. The
portrait was painted by Dyer's friend, Henry Meyer,
in 1819, one of the conditions being that Dyer's
favourite dog Daphne should be included.

(*From a picture in the
Fitzwilliam Museum*)

GEORGE DYER
with Daphne (*not* Tobit), his dog

no record of the speech, but anyone who has read Mr Birrell's *Obiter Dicta* or heard him speak will know how well he played his part. He told us of his adventures in Ireland in shaking hands with murderers, and in witnessing the result of the new weekly dole to old women in the villages, who bought gaudy motor veils to flaunt in the streets.

During the dinner the beautiful Christ's Hospital gold medal was passed round. It was given first in 1875, the centenary of Lamb's birth, for the English essay. Some unpublished letters in Lamb's handwriting were also brought by guests, and read with interest.

The late Sir Clifford Allbutt made a neat speech and congratulated us in having avoided all pomposity; one of us in reply agreed that by pomposity our Lamb-like spirit would be quite *cowed*.

¶ LATER DINNERS

The Second Dinner was perhaps even more successful than the first. The Master of Trinity, Dr H. M. Butler, presided and took charge of our guest, Mr E. V. Lucas, who read to us an interesting paper on Charles Lamb and Cambridge[1], and has lately sent the following vivid and humorous recollections of his entertainment:

[1] See p. 31.

August 1924.
78, Buckingham Gate,
On the Edge of Petty France,
S.W. 1.
To

George Wherry, *Esq.*,
5, St Peter's Terrace,
Cambridge.

Dear Mr Wherry, I was very sorry to read of
the death of Charles Sayle, whom I shall
always think of as the best kind of self-effacing
enthusiastic book-man. On the morning after the
Charles Lamb Dinner of 1910 I went round the
Trinity Library with him and Aldis Wright, and I
remember noticing with what reverence he came
to every treasure, although to handle them was,
I suppose, his constant task.

It has amused me, at this distance of fourteen
years, to set down such impressions as I retain of
that visit to Cambridge, hoping that they may
amuse you too.

I stayed on that occasion at Trinity College with
the Master, the late Dr Butler, and I was honoured
by being given a bedroom with historical associa-
tions of a somewhat formidable character, for a
brass plate recorded the fact that it had been once
occupied, many years before, by Queen Victoria
and her Consort. The footman who showed me to
it expressed the wish that I should not smoke as I
dressed; but he need not have troubled: I should

never have dreamed of so desecrating such a
sanctuary.

I had not yet seen the Master, whom I found
waiting in the hall ready to drive to the University
Arms Hotel in a brougham; and I was struck by
the disparity between his fine great authoritative
head, as of a Biblical patriarch, and the soft
caressing almost deferential voice.

And so we started for the slaughter, I nervous
as all public occasions—even so friendly a one as
this—make me, and not in the least fortified by
the circumstance that directly we arrived the
Master changed his boots; for I wondered if this
was one of those sacred Cambridge customs that
even strangers ought to know about; and I had
but the one pair I was wearing!

I was placed on the Master's right; and on my
other side were you, and I remember realising that
I had never met a student of Lamb with so much
knowledge, zeal and generosity. Later in the
evening I had some talk with one whose work I had
long admired and even fattened on—Dr Giles of the
Chinese Biographical Dictionary. I also met A. C.
Benson for the first time, in the not inconsiderable
flesh.

The actual dinner, which piously included sucking-
pig, would have been more alluring if the knowledge
was not weighing upon me that, as the guest of the
evening, I was after it to stand and deliver; but
the fact that I had prepared something which could
frankly be read made it possible to eat a mouthful
here and there and drink, with less difficulty, the
wine that you provided. The Suffragettes were then

at the height of their revolt, and I remember
creating, before I began to read, a fairly good im-
pression as one who knew his Lamb by suggesting
that if they carried out their threat to burn down
the Houses of Parliament, they should not waste
them but roast a pig or two in the process.

This joke going well, I started to read with the
more confidence, but my reading aloud is, as a
matter of fact, merely another way of keeping
matters secret; and the circumstance that the
Master was sleeping softly by my side did not heighten
my spirits. As the paper, however, was printed in
the following number of the *Cambridge Review*
(February 17th, 1910), under the title "Cambridge
and Charles Lamb," some idea of my drift in course
of time got about.

When I had finished reading, the Master made a
few apposite remarks in perfectly turned phrases,
which showed either that he could slumber with
one ear open or that years and years of familiarity
with public speakers had provided him with very
definite and accurate data as to their probable line
of attack.

On our return to the Lodge we found Bishop
Montgomery, another guest (also of Harrow and
Trinity) waiting up for us, in a room to which
tobacco might penetrate, and the Master, now wide
awake, the Bishop and I, sat on for an hour talking
not about Charles Lamb but about one of the few
subjects to which he never makes any reference
whatever, either in his works or correspondence—
cricket: a subject on which the Bishop is an
authority. As we talked, the Master, with perfect

urbanity, brought the conversation round to some verses of his own which I had unhappily misquoted in a recent book. The famous Harrow poem, in praise of Frederick Ponsonby and the Hon. Robert Grimston, begins thus:

"Old Damon and Old Pythias,
    They always found together;"

but I, being not an Harrovian but only a busybody, had changed the second line to:

"Were always found together."

I am glad of the error, because it led to a long digression on Harrow slang and other early reminiscences. The Master's references to cricket ranged from his school days to the banquet in honour of Ranjitsinhji at which he had taken the chair, and as usual, he seemed to know all.

The next morning Aldis Wright and Charles Sayle came to breakfast, and Aldis Wright filled me with complacency and pride by trusting me to take away the original exercise book in which Edward FitzGerald had written down his notes on Charles Lamb. I assure you that it was punctually returned.

I see from your list that Walter Raleigh was the guest of the evening in the following year. No one could speak about Charles Lamb better than he, and I have always regretted that the notes of an address he delivered at the *Times* Book Club were irrecoverable.

Believe me, dear Mr Wherry,
            Yours sincerely,
                    E. V. LUCAS.

Of the Master's speech introducing Mr Lucas
I recall that he thought the name of "Charles,"
always used in speaking of Lamb, was to some
extent a term of endearment, and mentioned
Charles Sayle and Charles Moule as modern
instances. He did not, however, give the
pathetic words of Lamb when Randal Norris
died: "to the last he called me Charley; I have
none to call me Charley now."

One of the souvenirs which was reproduced
by kind permission of the Master of Magdalene
[Dr Donaldson] and given to guests at the
Dinner is shown here.

Mr E. V. Lucas, to whom the text was sub-
mitted on its discovery in 1911, proved in an
article in the *Cambridge Review* for 7 June,
1911, that the letter was written in 1819, probably about August 15.

The following is taken from Mr Lucas's article:
"Last year the *Cambridge Review* printed
some notes of mine[1] on Charles Lamb and Cambridge in which I hazarded the conjecture that
when Lamb entitled a certain sonnet 'Written at
Cambridge, August 15, 1819,' he was indulging
once again in mystification. The little note
printed above[2] (for the first time) proves me to

---

[1] See p. 40.
[2] I.e. the letter here shown in facsimile.

Dear T. We are at Mr Bays's, Hatter,
Trumpington Street, Cambridge. Can you come down?
You will be with us, all but Bed, which you can get
at an Inn. We shall be most glad to see you.
Be so good as to send me Hazlitt's volume, just published, or
at Hones', directed as above. Or, much better, bring it

Yours, hic et ubique,

C Lamb

A letter from Lamb, probably written to Talfourd in 1819

have been too ingenious; for its evidence that
Lamb was in Cambridge in 1819 is as strong
as that which tells us he was there also in 1820.
The evidence is that the only book by Hazlitt
which Hone published was *Political Essays,
with Sketches of Public Characters*, printed by
William Hone, 45 Ludgate Hill, 1819. If then
Hazlitt's book determines the year, we may
take the testimony of the lately impugned
sonnet as to the month, especially as Lamb at
that time always took his holidays in the summer; and this gives us August: a peculiarly
satisfactory conclusion for Cambridge men, because it was on July 20, 1819, that Lamb received Miss Kelly's letter refusing his offer of
marriage, and the new little note that has just
come to light shows us that it was to Cambridge
that he thereupon went for comfort and solace.

The letter has still further value in adding
another Lamb domicile to the list, Mr Bays's
house being still in existence, although no longer
Trumpington Street, but King's Parade[1].

" 'T' I guess to have been Talfourd, who
had just been writing an enthusiastic review of
Lamb's *John Woodvill* in the *Champion*, and was
only too happy to serve his hero in any way."

[1] Mr Walter Bays has informed me that his
family has lived at 11 King's Parade since 1798. [Ed.]

In June 1913 we obtained permission from Corpus Christi College to place a suitable tablet on Bays's house.

The Third Dinner, in 1911, was presided over by Professor Henry Jackson, O.M.; our guest was Sir Walter Raleigh, Professor of English Literature at Oxford, and many look back with pleasure to his discourse. Our dinner was so far private that no reporter was present, and I regret that there is no record of his amusing speech, on a subject which entirely suited him. The guests took away with them a souvenir in the form of a photograph of Button Snap, Lamb's "only real property," about which Mr Lucas has written:

"In the month of August in the year 1812 Charles Lamb became a landed proprietor. He mentions the circumstances in the essay 'My First Play,' where writing of his godfather, Francis Fielde, he says: 'He is dead—and thus much I thought due to his memory, both for my first orders [for the Play] (little wondrous talismans! slight keys, and insignificant to our sight, but opening to me more than Arabian paradises!) and moreover, that by his testamentary beneficence I came into possession of the only landed property which I could ever

BUTTON SNAP

Charles Lamb's only real property
12 August 1812 – 25 February 1815

call my own—situate near the roadway village
of pleasant Puckeridge in Hertfordshire. When
I journeyed down to take possession, and
planted foot on my own ground, the stately
habits of the donor descended upon me, and I
strode (shall I confess the vanity?) with larger
paces over my allotment of three-quarters of
an acre, with its commodious mansion in the
midst, with the feeling of an English freeholder
that all betwixt sky and earth was my own.'
Francis Fielde left the property to his wife, who
conveyed it to Charles Lamb by indentures of
lease and release, dated August 20 and 21, 1812.
It is a cottage and garden situated at West
Hill Green in the parish of Buntingford in
Hertfordshire, about two-and-a-half miles from
Puckeridge. Mr Greg, the present owner, has
placed a tablet on the wall of the cottage stating
that Lamb once owned it. The little place can
have changed hardly at all since Francis
Fielde's godson made the momentous journey
to see his first and last freehold. Lamb's tenant
was a Mr Gargus and when Lamb sold the
property in 1815 for fifty pounds (Mr Fielde
had given twenty for it) he remitted the last
quarter's rent as a set-off against repairs.

"Mr Greg (whose ancestor Lamb called Grig)
believes that the name of the cottage, Button

Snap, was given to it by Lamb. This may be so; but I have lately heard of an old man who claimed to be related to a cousin of Charles Lamb named Eliza Button, and who was the possessor of two scrap-books in each of which Lamb had written an acrostic, one being on the name of Button.

"All efforts to trace the old man have failed, but it occurs to me that the odd title of Lamb's cottage (Button Snap) may have some family connection.

"In a letter to Joseph Hume, Lamb writes: 'But I am no freeholder (*fuimus Troës, fuit Ilium*), but I sold it for £50. If they'd accept a copy-holder, we clerks are naturally *copy-holders.*'"

Sir Francis Darwin took charge of the Fourth Dinner in 1912 and we were fortunate in securing as our guest Mr [now Sir] Edmund Gosse. The latter's own recollections of a Charles Lamb Dinner presided over by Swinburne are printed on p. 49.

At the Fifth Dinner Dr [now Sir] Arthur Shipley was our chairman, and Mr [now Sir] Henry Newbolt gave us a most interesting speech. Again there is no report preserved, but

in the *Cambridge Review* for 13 February, 1913,
it is recorded:

"There were roughly 60 people present at
the fifth annual Charles Lamb Dinner, held on
Saturday in the University Arms. The Master
of Christ's officiated as chairman, and Mr
Newbolt was the guest of the evening.

"Mr Newbolt in a witty speech contended
that it was impossible to educate everyone to
the highest appreciation of Literature and Art.
The most that could be done was to draw out
and develop within a man his own latent sense
of the beautiful.

"A momentary interruption was caused by
the setting on fire of a shade by its guttering
candle. It was bravely snatched from the
burning by a distinguished Cambridge musician
[Dr Alan Gray], who, not knowing how to deal
with the matter, handed the flaming paper to
his neighbour; the latter passed it on, and
the movement continued until someone [Dr
Guillemard] extinguished the fire with his
hands.

"'This is not,' remarked Mr Newbolt when
peace was restored, 'the University where the
candle was lit which proved so difficult to ex-
tinguish.'

"At the conclusion of the dinner the guests

passed into an adjoining room where general
conversation was continued to a late hour."

The Master of Christ's has very kindly given
me a reminiscence of this and of a previous
dinner:

"There is something peculiarly appropriate
in Charles Sayle's connection with the Lamb
Dinners, which he founded and organised. In
many respects Sayle and Lamb were very dis-
similar—Sayle was almost a teetotaller, Lamb
was not; Sayle was almost a vegetarian, Lamb
liked 'sucking pig.' But in their love for children, of learning, old books, and pleasant converse, their devotion to their sister, their quiet
and quaint humour, there was much in common
between our friend and the clerk at the East
India Office. A certain gentle whimsicality was
characteristic of both the Charles's.

"I attended one or two dinners and I even
presided at the one which was held the year
before the War, but I have never kept a diary
and my memory is beginning to—well, not to
react as readily as it did. But I *do* remember
the dinner at which the late Professor Sir
Walter Raleigh was present, because he told us
a story which I never heard before and which
I have never seen in print, though doubtless it
has appeared. It is well known that Carlyle

had a poor opinion of Lamb, in fact he says in a letter which need not have been published: 'Charles Lamb I sincerely believe to be in some considerable degree insane. A more pitiful, ricketty, gasping, staggering, stammering Tomfool I do not know.' Carlyle was often brutal and he was brutal about Lamb. Now Raleigh's story was this. The first, and I believe the only time, that Lamb met the sage of Chelsea, was at a great London mansion, I think Holland House, where there was a well-stocked aviary. The philosopher became so enthusiastic and so vocal over the beauties of the plumage of a golden pheasant that Charles Lamb broke out 'P-p-pray, Sir, are you a p-p-poulterer?'"

Hazlitt's portrait of Charles Lamb, reproduced as frontispiece to this volume, was chosen as a souvenir of the fifth dinner.

At the Sixth Annual Dinner Mr G. S. Street, as Examiner of Plays, may be said to have represented Lamb as a dramatic critic.

The late Sir Clifford Allbutt, in introducing Mr Street, said he foresaw the time when they might have no more to say about Lamb; and he suggested that other essayists might be made the theme of discourses at future Lamb dinners.

He meant essayists in the Lamb manner

rather than essayists in general; for it was obvious that there were many writers, such as Bacon and Johnson, to whom the label essayists must be conceded, but who have nothing in common with Lamb, and from whom one gets nothing of the feeling of intimate enjoyment which one associated with "Elia."

He thought that the biographical or auto-biographical element in the Lamb essays, and in those of Steele and Addison, for example, had much to do with their charm.

Mr Street said that he thought most lovers of Lamb must feel with him that any public discourse on that subject was an impossibility. The feeling that one had for Lamb was of such an intimate character that to speak about him to an audience, and in anything approaching a formal manner, was almost a profanation. He understood, however, that there was no desire on the part of the Committee to confine the speaker to the author with whose name the dinner was connected, and he proposed to offer a few remarks on the literature of the 'Nineties.

There appeared to be at the present time a great deal of interest and curiosity about the 'Nineties, and he found that most people seemed to connect that period of literary activity primarily with the late Oscar Wilde, and with the *Yellow Book.*

He thought that Henley and the men of the *Scots Observer* had a far greater influence on the literature of a period during which the essay greatly flourished.

At present the essay did not flourish. It was a form of literary expression which demanded a condition of peace and quiet; this the life of the present day was quite unable to provide.

Perhaps the telephone had something to do with it. At all events he saw no signs of the essay coming to the fore in the near future; and for enjoyment in that field it would probably be necessary to go to the past rather than to the present or to the future.

The sixth dinner souvenir was a reproduction
of the portrait of Mary Lamb, (oil painting,
$24'' \times 29''$), about which Mr Lionel Cust writes:
"I remember your portrait of Mary Lamb very
well. It seems to agree quite well with the
double portrait of Charles and Mary Lamb
which I got for the National Portrait Gallery,
which is certainly by F. S. Cary. I do not think
that anyone else could have painted Mary Lamb
at that age, as they lived secluded, with oc-
casional visits to the Carys. See my notice of
F. S. Cary in the *Dictionary of National Bio-
graphy*."

(*From a picture, attributed to F. S. Cary,*
in the possession of George Wherry, Esq.)

MARY LAMB

II

CAMBRIDGE AND
CHARLES LAMB

by
E. V. Lucas

¶ CAMBRIDGE AND CHARLES LAMB

CAMBRIDGE did more for Lamb than is perhaps recognised even here, where most
things are known, although Lamb did less for
Cambridge than he should have done—as we
shall see. Cambridge indeed played no small
part in his life, for it gave him not only his
intimacy with Manning, which brought forth
to their full for the first time, and at a very
critical time, his powers of humorous improvisa-
tion and led to some of the richest letters in the
language; but it also gave him his adopted
daughter Emma Isola, without whom his old
age, often sad enough as it was, would have been
sadder far.

Lamb's first link with Cambridge was Coleridge. Coleridge came hither—to Jesus College
—from Christ's Hospital and Lamb's company
in February, 1791. He left Cambridge (without
a degree) and returned to Lamb's company late
in 1794, and at once they set to writing sonnets
together. Lamb, I think, visited Cambridge in
Coleridge's time, staying with another Christ's
Hospitaller, Franklin; but of the date of this
visit we have no record.

His second link with Cambridge, I should say,
was George Dyer, who spent a large part of his

laborious life in compiling valuable if unexciting
works in connection with the University; but
that of course was indirect. Writing to Manning
in 1800, Lamb says:

> Send me some news from the *banks of Cam*, as
> the poets delight to speak, especially George Dyer,
> who has no other name, nor idea, nor definition
> of Cambridge—namely, its being a market-town,
> sending members to Parliament, never entered into
> his definition: it was and is, simply the banks of
> the Cam, or the fair Cam, as Oxford is the banks of
> the Isis, or the fair Isis.

Coleridge and Franklin having left, Lamb
would have had no Cambridge tie but for the
egregious but useful Charles Lloyd, who, after
quarrelling with Coleridge, defying his father,
and marrying against the advice of most of his
own and his wife's friends, had settled down
here in 1799 to study. Requiring a tutor, his
footsteps were led by a wise providence to a
strange mathematical recluse—famous in his
cups for his comic grimaces—named Thomas
Manning. Manning was then twenty-seven. He
had been at Caius from 1790 to 1795, but
objecting to oaths and tests he had not taken
his degree, and was now leading an odd, rumin-
ative, semi-industrious existence, and waiting
for his real purpose in life to be fulfilled: the

meeting with a poor London clerk, three years
his junior, named Charles Lamb, and by sym-
pathetic appreciation calling forth a wealth of
freakishness, sagacity, and wit, that otherwise
might never have been awakened.

Lamb and Manning were brought together
by Lloyd at Birmingham in 1799; it was much
the best deed of Lloyd's life; a friendship
sprang up instantly; Lloyd dropped out; and
the next time that Lamb visited Cambridge
it was as Manning's guest, Manning having
already stayed with Lamb in London and met
Coleridge. The return visit was postponed
again and again, but on December 27th, 1800,
Lamb was able to write in practically certain
terms:

Man of many snipes,—I will sup with thee, Deo
volente, et diabolo nolente, on Monday night, the
5th of January, in the new year, and crush a cup
to the infant century.

A word or two of my progress. Embark at six
o'clock in the morning, with a fresh gale, on a
Cambridge one-decker; very cold till eight at night;
land at St Mary's light-house, muffins and coffee
upon table (or any other curious production of
Turkey or both Indies), snipes exactly at nine,
punch to commence at ten, with *argument*; differ-
ence of opinion is expected to take place about
eleven; perfect unanimity, with some haziness and
dimness, before twelve.—N.B. My single affection

is not so singly wedded to snipes; but the curious
and epicurean eye would also take a pleasure in
beholding a delicate and well-chosen assortment of
teals, ortolans, the unctuous and palate-soothing
flesh of geese wild and tame, nightingales' brains,
the sensorium of a young sucking pig, or any other
Christmas dish, which I leave to the judgment of
you and the cook of Gonville.

Manning lived then over a barber's in St
Mary's Passage. The name was Crisp, which
Lamb preferred to call Crips. I have not the
number, but no doubt an old directory would
supply it and then we should know (if the
building still stands) yet another house in which
Lamb had been convivial[1].

Manning left Cambridge for Paris in 1801, to
study Chinese, and everyone here must remember that perfect example of fantastic humour
based on affection—Lamb's letter dissuading
him from settling in China. Before he definitely
left Europe, however, Manning seems to have
returned to Cambridge for a while, for in 1805
he sent Lamb a brawn, which Lamb, in his
acknowledgment, affected to consider was the
gift, not of Manning but of Richard Hopkins,
the cook of Caius. He writes:

[1] No. 3, St Mary's Passage (Messrs Leach & Sons,
1910).

At first, I thought of declining the present; but Richard knew my blind side when he pitched upon brawn. 'Tis of all my hobbies the supreme in the eating way....Brawn was a noble thought. It is not every common gullet-fancier that can properly esteem it. It is like a picture of one of the choice old Italian masters. Its gusto is of that hidden sort. As Wordsworth sings of a modest poet,— "you must love him, ere to you he will seem worthy of your love"; so brawn, you must taste it, ere to you it will seem to have any taste at all. But 'tis nuts to the adept: those that will send out their tongues and feelers to find it out. It will be wooed, and not unsought be won. Now, ham-essence, lobsters, turtle, such popular minions, absolutely *court you*, lay themselves out to strike you at first smack, like one of David's pictures...compared with the plain russet-coated wealth of a Titian or a Correggio....Such are the obvious glaring heathen virtues of a corporation dinner, compared with the reserved collegiate worth of brawn. Do me the favour to leave off the business which you may be at present upon, and go immediately to the kitchens of Trinity and Caius, and make my most respectful compliments to Mr Richard Hopkins, and assure him that his brawn is most excellent...I leave it to you whether you shall choose to pay him the civility of asking him to dinner while you stay in Cambridge, or in whatever other way you may best like to show your gratitude to *my friend*. Richard Hopkins, considered in many points of view, is a very extra-ordinary character. Adieu: I hope to see you to supper in London soon, where we will taste Richard's brawn, and drink his health in a cheerful but moderate cup. We have not many such men in any rank of life as Mr R. Hopkins.

Cambridge should be proud of that letter, because it contains what might be called the first draft—the seed at any rate—of the Dissertation on Roast Pig (which also we owe to Manning). You should be happy to know that it was the cook of Trinity Hall and Caius who first touched Lamb's palate and genius to these fine issues.

By the kindness of Mr George Wherry, I have before me one of Hopkins' advertisements in a Cambridge paper for February 9, 1806.

CAMBRIDGE BRAWN.

R. Hopkins, Cook of Trinity Hall and Caius College, begs leave to inform the Nobility, Gentry, &c., that he has now ready for sale, BRAWN, BRAWN HEADS & CHEEKS.

All orders will be thankfully received, and forwarded to any part of the kingdom.

With Manning, who left Cambridge for ever in 1805, went the last of the early ties; and it was not till 1815 that Lamb was here again, and then only by chance. We know all about it from a letter—to my mind almost a perfect letter—from Mary Lamb to Miss Hutchinson, a large part of which I propose to read. The date is August 20, 1815:

Last Saturday was the grand feast day of the

India House Clerks. I think you must have heard
Charles talk of his yearly turtle feast. He had been
lately much wearied with work, and, glad to get
rid of all connected with it, he *used* Saturday, the
feast day being a holiday, *borrowed* the Monday
following, and we set off from the outside of the
Cambridge Coach from Fetter Lane at eight o'clock,
and were driven into Cambridge in great triumph
by Hell Fire Dick five minutes before three. Richard
is in high reputation, he is private tutor to the
Whip Club....

In my life I never spent so many pleasant hours
together as I did at Cambridge. We were walking
the whole time—out of one College into another.
If you ask me which I like best I must make the
children's traditionary unoffending reply to all
curious enquirers—"*Both.*" I liked them all best.
The little gloomy ones, because they were little
gloomy ones. I felt as if I could live and die in them
and never wish to speak again. And the fine grand
Trinity College, oh how fine it was! And King's
College Chapel, what a place! I heard the Cathedral
service there, and having been no great church goer
of late years, *that* and the painted windows and
the general effect of the whole thing affected me
wonderfully.

I certainly like St John's College best. I had seen
least of it, having only been over it once, so, on the
morning we returned, I got up at six o'clock and
wandered into it by myself—by myself indeed, for
there was nothing alive to be seen but one cat, who
followed me about like a dog. Then I went over
Trinity, but nothing hailed me there, not even a cat.

On the Sunday we met with a pleasant thing.
We had been congratulating each other that we
had come alone to enjoy, as the miser his feast, all
our sights greedily to ourselves, but having seen all
we began to grow flat and wish for this and t'other
body with us, when we were accosted by a young
gownsman whose face we knew, but where or how
we had seen him we could not tell, and were obliged
to ask his name. He proved to be a young man we
had seen twice at Alsager's. He turned out a very
pleasant fellow—shewed us the insides of places—
we took him to our Inn to dinner, and drank tea
with him in such a delicious College room, and then
again he supped with us. We made our meals as
short as possible, to lose no time, and walked our
young conductor almost off his legs. Even when
the fried eels were ready for supper and coming up,
having a message from a man who he had bribed
for the purpose, that then we might see Oliver
Cromwell [Cooper's portrait] who was *not at home*
when we called to see him, we sallied out again and
made him a visit by candlelight—and so ended our
sights. When we were setting out in the morning
our new friend came to bid us good bye, and rode
with us as far as Trumpington. I never saw a
creature so happy as he was the whole time he was
with us, he said we had put him in such good spirits
that [he] should certainly pass an examination well
that he is to go through in six weeks in order to
qualify himself to obtain a fellowship.

(What a pity we have not his letter too!)

Returning home down old Fetter Lane I could

hardly keep from crying to think it was all over.
With what pleasure [Charles] shewed me Jesus
College where Coleridge was—the barbe[r's shop]
where Manning was—the house where Lloyd lived
—Franklin's rooms, a young schoolfellow with
whom Charles was the first time he went to Cambridge: I peeped in at his window, the room looked
quite deserted—old chairs standing about in disorder that seemed to have stood there ever since
they had sate in them. I write sad nonsense about
these things, but I wish you had heard Charles talk
his nonsense over and over again about his visit to
Franklin and how he then first felt himself com-
mencing gentleman and had eggs for his breakfast.

Lamb, finding a spare inch or two, added a
few words before he sealed it:

"Dear Miss Hutchinson," he wrote: "I subscribe
most willingly to all my sister says of her Enjoyment at Cambridge. She was in silent raptures all
the while *there*, and came home riding thro' the air
(her 1st long outside journey), triumphing as if she
had been *graduated*. I remember one foolish-pretty
expression she made use of, 'Bless the little churches
how pretty they are,' as those symbols of civilised
life opened upon her view one after the other on
this side Cambridge. You cannot proceed a mile
without starting a steeple, with its little patch of
villagery round it, enverduring the waste."

So far we have been dealing with fact. Now
sets in the apocryphal era. In the *Examiner* for
August 29 and 30, 1819, appeared a sonnet by

Lamb entitled, "Written at Cambridge," and
dated August 15, 1819. It begins thus:

> I was not train'd in Academic bowers,
> And to those learned streams I nothing owe
> Which copious from those twin fair founts do flow;
> Mine have been any thing but studious hours.
> Yet can I fancy, wandering 'mid thy towers,
> Myself a nurseling, Granta, of thy lap;
> My brow seems tightening with the Doctor's cap,
> And I walk *gownèd*; feel unusual powers.

That sounds all right, does it not? Yet the fact
that Lamb entitled a sonnet "Written at Cambridge," and dated it there means—as any of
his editors will support me sadly in saying—
nothing at all. That was his way. Mystification
was as dear to his heart as metaphysics to
Coleridge, or mathematics to Manning, or orders
for brawn to Richard Hopkins. My own im-
pression is that that sonnet was written in
London any time between 1809 and 1819; and
that the statement "Written at Cambridge,"
and the circumstantial date have no value at
all. I can prove the reasonableness of this
suspicion only too easily by reminding you that
it was when Lamb was next really here—in
Trumpington Street, in July and August, 1820
—that he wrote his Elia essay called "Oxford
in the Vacation," dating it August 5, 1820,

from his rooms "facing the Bodleian," and
stating how he met, in a nook at Oriel, George
Dyer, who, as a matter of fact, was then en-
gaged on his work on Cambridge privileges, and
was practically chained to Cambridge libraries;
and stating also, in the *London Magazine* version, how he had seen the Milton MS in the
Trinity Library, and did not like it! Why
Lamb should have affected to be at Oxford and
not at Cambridge only he could explain—and I
wish he was here to do so.

To the best of my knowledge he was at Oxford
only twice in his life—once in 1800, with Gutch,
and once in 1809, with Hazlitt. And Hazlitt, it
is worth noting, remarks on the fact (in the
essay "On the Conversation of Authors") that
among Oxford's courts and colleges Lamb
seemed to "walk gownèd"—quoting from the
Cambridge sonnet.

It was on the authenticated and very eventful
visit to Cambridge in July and August, 1820,
when Lamb and his sister were here for a
month, that they met the little girl named
Emma Isola, who was destined, as their adopted
daughter, to bring into their house so much
brightness and pleasure. The Lambs stayed
with or near a Mrs Paris, a sister of their London
friend, Ayrton, in Trumpington Street. Living

either there, or at Mrs Watford's, a house which they visited, was this attractive child; the brother and sister took an instant liking to her; the following January—1821—Emma was their guest in London, at Great Russell Street; and after her father's death in 1823 she passed into the charge of her new friends and remained with them, when not at school or teaching, until she became the wife of Moxon, the publisher, in 1833, and left their home, on which the shadows were gathering so fast, for ever.

Emma Isola's father was Charles Isola, of Emmanuel, an Esquire Bedell of the University; her grandfather was Agostino Isola, an Italian tutor here, among whose pupils was Wordsworth.

If we are to be chronological I must now mention one other Cambridge association bewilderingly tacked on to Oxford by its capricious chronicler. In the *London Magazine* for December, 1822, appeared an amusing character sketch by Lamb entitled "The Gentle Giantess," a farcical description of the Widow Blackett, an immensely corpulent Oxford lady, who was wont to sit in her cellar in the dog days, or amid draughts which gave her friends neuralgia, and who took the air in the evenings in Magdalen Grove. In writing to Dorothy Wordsworth in 1821, when she was staying at Trinity

Lodge, with her uncle, Christopher Wordsworth,
one of Dr Butler's predecessors, Lamb says:

Ask anybody you meet, who is the biggest
woman in Cambridge and I'll hold you a wager
they'll say Mrs Smith. She broke down two benches
in Trinity Gardens, one on the confines of St John's,
which occasioned a litigation between the societies
as to repairing it. In warm weather she retires into
an ice-cellar (literally!), and dates the returns of
the years from a hot Thursday some twenty years
back. She sits in a room with opposite doors and
windows, to let in a thorough draught, which gives
her slenderer friends tooth-aches.

That Lamb met Mrs Smith at Cambridge in
1820 we know, because Crabb Robinson, who
was on circuit here at the time, joined them in
a rubber. But what a man to edit!

And there Lamb's association with Cambridge
ends, unless we count his intimacy with William
Frend and his daughter Sophie Frend (afterwards Mrs Augustus De Morgan and mother of
the author of *Joseph Vance*) as another bond.

After so much minutiæ and confusion the
time has perhaps come to recapitulate. Briefly,
then, we find that Lamb probably first visited
Cambridge previous to the end of 1794, when
Coleridge left. His next visit was to Manning
in 1801. His next with his sister in Hell Fire
Dick's coach in 1815. So far we deal with facts.

Next comes the doubtful sojourn of August, 1819, providing the Cambridge sonnet[1]. Next the authenticated visit of a month in July and August, 1820, leading to the essay whimsically transferred to Oxford, and to the account of Mrs Smith, of Cambridge, as Oxford's Widow Blackett; and leading also to the adoption of Emma Isola.

Both therefore in Lamb's work and life Cambridge may be said to have no little share; and although it gave him Manning's stimulating intellectual heartiness at a time when he needed it, most of all are you, I think, to be felicitated with for providing for his many lonely hours after his retirement from the India House that merry and sensible girl who was to be so valuable a companion and a friend—that "girl of gold," as he called her, that "silent brown girl": silent, and yet at the same time, as he said, the "best female talker" he had ever known.

It was with mixed feelings that Lamb gave his consent for her marriage to Edward Moxon in 1833. Mary Lamb's attacks were becoming more frequent and acute; his own health was failing; his home was, he knew only too well, no place for a girl on the threshold of life. A few months after the wedding he wrote a letter to

[1] But see pp. 18, 19.

both husband and wife, which seems to me not
the least courageous effort of a noble and
courageous life. It begins with criticism—for
Moxon had the sonnet habit very badly—and
incidentally Lamb urges him to quarrel with
his wife whenever he can, for she is "beautiful
in reconciliation." And then he describes how
he has been lured once again into an excess of
conviviality, such as Emma had so often—and,
I feel, so understandingly—deplored. He adds—

"Tell it not in Gath, Emma, lest the daughters
triumph!" I am at the end of my tether. I wish
you would come on Tuesday with your fair bride.
Why can't you. Do... Come and bring a sonnet on
Mary's birthday. Love to the whole Moxonry, and
tell E. I every day love her more, and miss her less.

Miss her less! Never, if truth is to be told, did
he miss her more or need her more. It was
another of those white lies which Cambridge
fostered in him; another absolute inversion of
the fact; Oxford for Cambridge once again: but
what a fine brave tragic falsehood!

E. V. LUCAS.

It is interesting to note that Cambridge now
possesses the best portrait of George Dyer (with
his dog) that exists. It was bequeathed to the
Masters and Scholars of the University by Miss
Sarah Travers and hangs in the Fitzwilliam Museum.
See p. 12.

III

THE EARLIEST
CHARLES LAMB
DINNER

by

Sir Edmund Gosse

¶ THE EARLIEST CHARLES LAMB DINNER

YOUR invitation to me to be present to-night at the Fourth Annual Dinner given at Cambridge in honour of Charles Lamb's birthday, was one which flattered me not a little; and to-night I am still more gratified to find myself surrounded by so many distinguished leaders of Cambridge thought.

I do not know what could be more touching to my feelings than to stand here, in the midst of the University from which I have received so much, and to which my gratitude and loyalty are due in no ordinary measure, while I enjoy the reception which you have just given to my old friend Francis Darwin's too kind and too indulgent introduction of my name.

This day, the 10th of February, is the 137th anniversary of the birth of Charles Lamb, a date now celebrated every year in Cambridge, the University for which he entertained—it is true, at a considerable distance—an almost idolatrous veneration. Every year renews the old love, the old enthusiasm, as is proper when the source of them is so perennial, yet we may concede that the 137th anniversary must be counted among the minor festivals of the Agnine Church. I will, if you will allow me,

tell you something about a major festival, at
which I had the good fortune to be present, but
which hardly anyone else can possibly remember. I will describe to you the first Charles
Lamb Dinner which ever was held, on the 100th
anniversary of his birth. At that time—nearly
forty years ago, alas!—it was my privilege to
be in close relations of friendship with that great
poet and very fine gentleman, Algernon Charles
Swinburne.

He had lodgings in London, but town life
never suited him, and particularly in the
winter it was his habit to spend several months
at a time, usually from October to February,
with his parents at Holmwood, their house near
Henley-on-Thames. Hence, I had in those
years not merely the advantage of seeing him
very frequently through the spring and summer,
but of receiving his delightful letters at other
times. Soon after the beginning of 1875 I had
happened to point out in one of my letters
that he had allowed the centenary of Walter
Savage Landor's birth to pass unnoticed. Centenaries commonly did pass unnoticed in those
days. In his reply (Jan. 30) Swinburne expressed himself extremely vexed that he should
have missed this historical landmark, but
pointed out to me that, in less than a fortnight,

another event would take place, the anniversary
of Charles Lamb's birth. He suggested that
we might commemorate with the same libations,
both the great men, who loved and admired
each other in life, and whose memories he
thought might fitly and gracefully be mingled
after death in our affectionate recollection.

Accordingly he undertook to organise what he
called "our Passover feast in honour of a Lamb
quite other than Paschal," and proposed to
come up to town specially for the purpose of
making arrangements. I think it was the only
time in his whole life that Swinburne ever
"organised" anything; he was not gifted in
a practical direction. However he took the
Charles Lamb dinner very seriously, and came
to town on Monday, the 8th, to settle all the
details. He would not allow me to help him at
all; "Leave it to me!" he said, in his grandest
manner. You will hear, with surprise, that the
dinner did come off. It was a rough entertainment, and the guests were few, but it did come off.

I can, without any difficulty, name the con-
vives. There was Swinburne, of course, at the
head of the table, looking very small in an
immense armchair, but preserving a mien of
rare solemnity. There was our dear and ever-
cheerful William Minto, of Aberdeen, who left

us so prematurely nineteen years ago; there
was a rather trying journalist, Purnell, who
has also long been dead, and there were Mr
Theodore Watts (now Watts-Dunton) and myself. That was the company, fit, perhaps, but
certainly few. We met in a very old-fashioned
hotel in Soho, and had a coarse, succulent
dinner in the mid-Victorian style, very much
I dare say in Charles Lamb's own taste.

The extreme dignity of Swinburne was the
feature of the dinner which remains chiefly in
my memory; he sank so low in his huge arm-
chair, and sat so bolt upright in it, his white
face, with its great aureole of red hair, beaming
over the table like the rising sun. It was
magnificent to see Swinburne, when Purnell,
who was a reckless speaker, "went too far,"
bringing back the conversation into the paths
of decorum. He was a perfect Mrs Grundy. He
was so severe, so unwontedly and phenomenally
severe, that Purnell sulked, and taking out a
churchwarden, left us at table and smoked in
the chimney-corner. Our shock was the bill—
portentous! Swinburne in "organising" had
made no arrangement as to price, and when we
trooped out into the frosty midnight, there were
five long faces of impecunious men of letters.
This dinner, which contrasted in every way so

disadvantageously with the feast of to-night,
was almost a complete innovation at that date.
No one thought of celebrating centenaries, and
now, nearly forty years later, some people hold
that we think of them too much. I am not one
of those. I delight in occasions on which we
meet to recall to our memories those illustrious
lamp-bearers who have preceded us on the way.
I think it is easy to justify these anniversaries.
They are not idle meetings; they serve to re-
mind us of the stages in the long evolution of
art. The great poets, the great prose-writers,
are, in my idea, not teachers so much as
magicians. There is something supernatural
about them. They laboured while they were
alive to illuminate for us the prodigious image
of the world as the eternal source of joy and
sorrow. What they wrote, and more than that,
what they were, what they said, the legend
that gathers around them, loses (as we retreat
from it) all that is sordid, all that is of the
earth, earthy, and takes a luminous and
heavenly tinge. What literature and art do is
to bring harmony and happiness into this
universe of grief and disorder; and centenaries,
anniversaries, what you will, are occasions for
liberating ourselves from the bondage of the
present, and renewing our rapture.

This is the main benefit and peculiar value of anniversaries. I think less of the honour done to the illustrious person, although that is a fitting and a decent service.

But while our feast to-night does no good to Charles Lamb—that is to say, cannot be conceived to illuminate his genius or add to its lustre—it does good to each and all of us, in so far as, while delivering ourselves up to it, we reflect in common on his merit and excellence. There are few things more touching than that record in the Prophet Malachi of those "who spoke often one to another."

Let us speak often one to another of those things which elevate and charm us, and so the book of remembrance will be kept open. We are surrounded by influences which take us away from things of the spirit; we yield to the siren voices from the rocks of life, the inevitable tendencies to languor and giving up. I often think that the name and memory of a great man, with some unaffected discussion of his work, make a sovereign talisman against the relinquishment of the fight.

Yet at a dinner consecrated to the memory of Charles Lamb I have said nothing about his life or his works. But these are known to you all and are engraven on a brass that needs no futile burnishing of mine. I must claim, too, that though we have said little definite about the hero of to-day, his presence has been with us. For myself, I am almost persuaded that I have been conscious in our midst of some phantom of the wise and gentle Elia. And now, without further preamble, I beg you to drink with enthusiasm to the toast of the evening, the Immortal Memory of Charles Lamb.

IV

GEORGE DYER AND "DYER'S FREND"

by
George Wherry

The portrait of George Dyer (oil painting,
24″×20″) reproduced here has this interesting
record written on the back of the canvas in
three different handwritings:

This portrait of *Lamb's* George Dyer by [John]
Jackson R.A. was presented by Dyer to his most
intimate friend William Frend of Jesus College
Cambridge M.A. and S.W. Celebrated in his day
and now 1891 belongs to his son Henry Tyrwhitt
Frend Barrister at law and now to W. W. Frend
1896.

It went to National Portrait Exhibition as
Portrait of George Dyer (Jackson) lent by H. T.
Frend, Garden Court Temple.

GEORGE DYER

A considerable portion of the essay on George Dyer is taken from Mr Lucas's *Life of Charles Lamb*. I deeply regret that, owing to an oversight, the source of these borrowed passages was not fully acknowledged.

G. W.

[59]

ℭ GEORGE DYER

WHEN good Americans come to Cambridge they visit Emmanuel College, as being the college of Harvard. The best of these visitors will ask for memorials of George Dyer and these notes may enable them to climb "Parnassus" and discover his old rooms[1].

At Christ's Hospital, which he entered in 1762 at the age of seven, Dyer came under the influence of Dr Anthony Askew, who had taken his degree of M.B. at Emmanuel in 1745 and combined the practice of medicine in Cambridge with much European travel, and a passion for classical scholarship.

From Cambridge Askew went to London, and of him was written the childish rhyme

"What's Doctor, and Dr and *Doctor* writ so?

Doctor Long, Dr Short and Doctor Askew."

He was Physician to St Bartholomew's Hospital, and was one of the owners of the famous gold-headed cane which was given by Radcliffe to Mead, by Mead to Askew, passed to Pitcairn

[1] The account of Dyer's life at school and college is based on material mostly given to me by the late J. B. Peace, Fellow of Emmanuel and University Printer.

and Baillie, and given by Joanna Baillie to the College of Physicians. Dyer was much indebted to this Dr Askew for introductions to the learned world of Cambridge and London.

Dyer was entered as a sizar at Emmanuel in 1774. He learnt his classics under Richard Dawes of Newcastle School, but, probably on account of poverty, did not actually begin college life until two years later.

William Taylor, who was to become Dyer's closest undergraduate friend, came up from Cumberland in the same year. They occupied the two small sets of rooms known as "Parnassus," at the top of the "staircase next the fields," now Staircase G in the brick building; Dyer having the left-hand set "looking over the fields." Farmer was then tutor, but in the following year succeeded Dr Richardson in the Mastership. The work of tutor was mainly in the hands of William Bennet, afterwards Bishop of Cloyne. Him Dyer called "my learned Tutor."

When Farmer died in 1797 Dyer wrote a memoir, which appeared in the Annual Necrology. He points out that it was natural that Farmer, coming up to a Tory college, should adopt principles he so consistently professed in later life; and "fortunately for him," he says, "these principles proved favourable to his future advancement."

If by opposing academical reforms, says Dyer, he kept back intellectual light, if by resisting the spirit of liberty he lessened the sum of human happiness, yet let posterity give him due praise;... as he was the principal mover in getting the town lighted and paved....

Askew, being a man of the world, continued to help Dyer with introductions which gave him "large and intimate acquaintance with learned members of the University." William Taylor, Dyer's real friend, was an excellent mathematician—second wrangler in 1778, when Farish, afterwards Jacksonian Professor, was senior. The two, though rivals, were close friends, and Dyer was intimate with both. Taylor was elected Fellow in 1780. Another friend of Dyer's was the notorious Gilbert Wakefield of Jesus. Wakefield was second wrangler in 1776. Says the modern historian of Jesus, "Wakefield's memoirs give a measure of the man's garrulity, inconsequence and vanity. Alike in politics, religion and scholarship he showed himself altogether lacking in discretion."

He at least paid the price, spending two years in Dorchester gaol for expressing, in a

theological pamphlet, the wish that the French
Revolutionists might invade and conquer Eng-
land. His defects were not unknown to his
friends and may be covered by their charity.
Dyer goes on:

I purposely avoid entering into nice discrimination of character, either in way of panegyric or
censure. But of an estimable friend, well known
by many years' intimacy, I must be permitted to
add, that whatever apparent asperities occur in
his writings, they never passed into his private life.
There he was eminently amiable and mild.

The second wrangler of 1780 was also a friend
of Dyer. This was William Frend of Christ's,
of whom some account is given later.

In 1800 Frend, Dyer and one or two others
of like mind founded "A Literary Club or
Association" for purposes of literary and scien-
tific discussion. The meetings took place at the
Chapter Coffee House in Paternoster Row, and
the club was known as the Chapter Coffee
House Club.

Among the members were Samuel Rogers,
the banker-poet; Maltby, Librarian of the
British Museum; Shee, afterwards P.R.A.;
Henry Tresham, R.A.; John Hoppner, R.A.;
Dr John Aiken; and "Conversation Sharpe,"
the versatile hatter from Fenchurch Street.

[63]

The painters of the day took kindly to literature.
Lamb, in a letter to Dyer in 1808, says of them:

How these painters encroach on our province!
There's Hoppner, Shee, Westall, and I don't know
who besides, and Tresham. It seems on confession,
that they are not at the top of their own art, when
they seek to eke out their fame with the assistance
of another's; no large tea-dealer sells cheese, no
great silversmith sells razor-strops; it is only
your petty dealers who mix commodities. If Nero
had been a great Emperor, he would never have
played the Violoncello. Who ever caught you,
Dyer, designing a landscape, or taking a likeness?

Dyer entered the family of Robert Robinson
of Cambridge, the Baptist minister who afterwards turned to Unitarianism. That "valiant
Dissenter" was then living at Chesterton with
his numerous children, to whom G. D. was to
act as tutor. At that time Dyer was fully in-
tending to take orders, as all Grecians were
expected to do, but under Robinson's influence
he too became a Unitarian and gave up his
ecclesiastical projects.

Robinson, a sensible and humorous man of
strong individuality, died in 1790, leaving Dyer
to edit his *History of Baptism*, and his *Ecclesiastical Researches*, and then to write his life in
1796—a book which Wordsworth called "one
of the best biographies in the language." Change

of faith having brought his intended career to
an end, Dyer returned to teaching after Robinson's death, and it was then that he joined
Dr Ryland in a school at Northampton, where
he had for a colleague John Clarke, father of
Lamb's friend, Charles Cowden Clarke. That
was in 1791. While at Northampton, at the
age of thirty-six, he knew, perhaps for the first
and last time, Romance. Like Calverley's
"Gemini," both G. D. and John Clarke loved
the same lady, the Rev. Dr Ryland's step-
daughter. Clarke won her, but the two rivals
continued friends; and "many years after,"
writes Cowden Clarke, "when my father died,
George Dyer asked for a private conference
with me, told me of his youthful attachment
for my mother, and enquired whether her circumstances were comfortable, because in case,
as a widow, she had not been left well off he
meant to offer her his hand. Hearing that in
point of money she had no cause for concern,
he begged me to keep secret what he had con-
fided to me, and himself never made further
allusion to the subject." I think that is one of
the prettiest stories I know; and it lends em-
phasis to Hazlitt's remark of G. D. in his essay
in 1824, "On the look of a Gentleman" (Dyer
being the common property of the essayists),

that he was one of "God Almighty's gentle-men."

In 1792, making up his mind as to his true vocation, Dyer turned his steps to London and took the rooms in Clifford's Inn from which he never moved. There he dwelt, as Lamb said, "like a dove in an asp's nest," and began his long career as a hack and the friend of letters and men of letters. Dyer's principal work was scholarly and serious; but he had his lighter moments too, when he wrote verses, some of them quite sprightly, and moved sociably from house to house. In a letter from Lamb to Wordsworth some years later:

To G. D. a poem is a poem. His own as good as anybody's, and (God bless him!) anybody's as good as his own: for I do not think he has the most distant guess of the possibility of one poem being better than another. The gods by denying him the very faculty itself of discrimination, have effectu-ally cut off every seed of envy in his bosom.

Dyer's principal verses are to be found in his *Poems*, 1801. This book originally was to con-sist of two volumes, one containing poetry and the other criticism; but its author altered and changed his plan, and it was ultimately sent to the printer in one volume with sixty-eight pages of preface.

And then occurred a tragedy; for just after
the book was ready Dyer suddenly realised that
he had committed himself in this preface to a
principle in which he did not really believe.
Lamb tells the story in a letter to Manning in
December, 1800:

At length George Dyer's phrenesis has come to a
crisis: he is raging and furiously mad. I waited
upon the heathen, Thursday was a se'nnight; the
first symptom which struck my eye and gave me
incontrovertible proof of the fatal truth was a pair
of nankeen pantaloons four times too big for him,
which the said Heathen did pertinaciously affirm
to be new. They were absolutely ingrained with the
accumulated dirt of ages; but he affirmed them to
be clean. He was going to visit a lady that was
nice about those things, and that's the reason he
wore nankeen that day. And then he danced, and
capered, and fidgeted, and pulled up his pantaloons, and hugged his intolerable flannel vestment
closer about his poetic loins; anon he gave it loose
to the zephyrs which plentifully insinuate their
tiny bodies through every crevice, door, window or
wainscot, expressly formed for the exclusion of such
impertinents. Then he caught at a proof sheet, and
catched up a laundress's bill instead—made a dart
at Blomfield's Poems, and threw them in agony
aside. I could not bring him to one direct reply;
he could not maintain his jumping mind in a right
line for the tithe of a moment by Clifford's Inn
clock. He must go to the printer's immediately—

the most unlucky accident—he had struck off five hundred impressions of his Poems, which were ready for delivery to subscribers, and the Preface must all be expunged. There were eighty pages of Preface, and not till that morning had he discovered that in the very first page of said Preface he had set out with a principle of Criticism fundamentally wrong, which vitiated all his following reasoning. The Preface must be expunged, although it cost him £30—the lowest calculation, taking in paper and printing! In vain have his real friends remonstrated against this Midsummer madness. George is as obstinate as a Primitive Christian—and wards and parries off all our thrusts with one unanswerable fence—"Sir, it's of great consequence that the *world* is not *misled!*"

A few months later George Dyer's phrenesis came to a head again. Lamb told the story to Rickman, to whom Dyer had introduced him, in a letter of which, in the part appertaining to Dyer, I cannot bring myself to curtail a syllable:

I wish I could convey to you any notion of the whimsical scenes I have been witness to in this fortnight past. 'Twas on Tuesday week the poor heathen scrambled up to my door about breakfast time. He came thro' a violent rain with no neck-cloth on, and a *beard* that made him a spectacle to men and angels, and tap'd at the door. Mary open'd it, and he stood stark still and held a paper in his hand importing that he had been ill with a fever. He either wouldn't or couldn't speak except by signs. When you went to comfort him he put his hand upon his heart and shook his head, and told us his complaint lay where no medicines could reach it. I was dispatch'd for Dr Dale, Mr Phillips of St Paul's Churchyard and Mr Frend who is to be his executor. George solemnly delivered into Mr Frend's hands and mine an old burnt preface that had been in the fire, with injunctions which we solemnly vow'd to obey that it should be printed after his death with his last corrections, and that some account should be given to the world why he had not fulfill'd his engagement with subscribers. Having done this and borrow'd two guineas of his bookseller (to whom he imparted in confidence that he should leave a great many loose papers behind him which would only want methodizing and arranging to prove very lucrative to any bookseller after his death) he laid himself down on my bed in a mood of complacent resignation.

By the aid of meat and drink put into him (for I all along suspected a vacuum) he was enabled to sit up in the evening, but he had not got the better of his intolerable fear of dying; he expressed such philosophic indifference in his speech and such frightened apprehensions in his physiognomy that if he had truly been dying, and I had known it, I could not have kept my countenance.

In particular when the doctor came and ordered him to take little white powders (I suppose of chalk or alum, to humour him) he ey'd him with a *suspicion* which I could not account for; he has since explain'd that he took it for granted Dr Dale

knew his situation and had ordered him these
powders to hasten his departure that he might
suffer as little pain as possible.

Think what an aspect the heathen put on with
these fears upon a dirty face. To recount all his
freaks for two or three days while he thought he
was going, and how the fit operated, and sometimes the man got uppermost and sometimes the
author, and he had this excellent person to serve,
and he must correct some proof sheets for Phillips,
and he could not bear to leave his subscribers
unsatisfy'd, but he must not think of these things
now, he was going to a place where he should
satisfy all his debts—and when he got a little better
he began to discourse what a happy thing it would
be if there was a place where all the good men and
women in the world might meet, meaning heav'n,
and I really believe for a time he had doubts about
his soul, for he was very near, if not quite, light
headed. The fact was that he had not had a good
meal for some days, and his little dirty Niece
(whom he sent for with a still dirtier Nephew, and
hugg'd him; and bid them farewell) told us that
unless he dines out he subsists on tea and gruels.

And he corroborated this tale by ever and anon
complaining of sensations of gnawing which he felt
about his *heart*, which he mistook his stomach to
be, and sure enough these gnawings were dissipated
after a meal or two, and he surely thinks that he
has been rescued from the jaws of death by Dr
Dale's white powders.

He is got quite well again by nursing, and chirps
of odes and lyric poetry the day long—he is to go

out of town on Monday, and with him goes the
dirty train of his papers and books which follow'd
him to our house. I shall not be sorry when he
takes his nipt carcase out of my bed, which it has
occupied, and vanishes with all his Lyric lumber,
but I will endeavour to bring him in future into a
method of dining at least once a day. I have
proposed to him to dine with me—and he has
nearly come into it whenever he does not go out
—and pay me. I will take his money before hand
and he shall eat it out. If I don't it will go all over
the world. Some worthless relations, of which the
dirty little devil that looks after him and a still
more dirty nephew are component particles, I have
reason to think divide all his gains with some worthless authors that are his constant satellites. The
Literary Fund has voted him seasonably £20, and
if I can help it he shall spend it on his own carcase.
I have assisted him in arranging the remainder of
what he calls Poems....

What do you think of a life of G. Dyer? I can
scarcely conceive a more amusing novel. He has
been connected with all sects in the world and he
will faithfully tell all he knows. Every body will
read it; and if it is not done according to my fancy,
I promise to put him in a novel when he dies.
Nothing shall escape *me*. If you think it feasible,
whenever you write you may encourage him. Since
he has been so close with me I have perceiv'd the
workings of his inordinate vanity, his gigantic
attention to particles and to prevent open vowels
in his odes, his solicitude that the public may not
lose any tittle of his poems by his death, and all

the while his utter ignorance that the world don't
care a pin about his odes and his criticisms, a fact
which every body knows but himself—he *is a rum
genius.*

Lamb's idea of putting Dyer into a novel was
not a new one. Writing to Coleridge in 1800
he had said:

George Dyer is the only literary character I am
happily acquainted with. The oftener I see him the
more deeply I admire him. He is goodness itself.
If I could but calculate the precise date of his
death, I would write a novel on purpose to make
George the hero. I could hit him off to a hair.

If only the novel had been written! But
there could be nothing in it better than the
letter to Rickman.

A letter to Rickman on November 24th, 1801,
shows that Dyer was conforming to Lamb's
plans for him:

Dyer regularly dines with me when he does not
go a visiting—and brings his shilling. He has
picked up amazingly. I never saw him happier.
He has had his doors listed, and his casements
puttied, and bought a handsome screen of the last
century. Only his poems do not get finished. One
volume is printing, but the second wants a good
deal doing to it.
I do not expect he will make much progress
with his Life and Opinions till his detestable Lyric
Poetry is delivered to subscribers....He talks of

marrying, but this *en passant* (as he says) and *entre nous*, for God's sake don't mention it to him, for he has not forgiven me for betraying to you his purpose of writing his own Life. He says, that if it once spreads, so many people will expect and wish to have a place in it, that he is sure he shall disoblige all his friends.

Dyer, it seems, did write his autobiography, but the MS was lost.

Mr Lucas writes:

I wonder which of his poems Dyer read to the other patients at Dr Graham's earth-bath establishment (as he did when he was being treated there), his audience, like himself, being half buried in the gardens all around him? What a picture?

Best among Dyer's prose works were the *Memoirs of the Life and Writings of Robert Robinson* and his *History of the University of Cambridge*. He wrote moreover countless articles, memoirs and biographies for periodicals, pamphlets on religious questions, and "all that was original" in James Valpy's edition of the classics in 141 volumes, 1809–1831.

The essay, "Oxford in the Vacation," contains Lamb's delightful account of meeting Dyer at "Oxford" (really at Cambridge), "grown almost into a book" among the books he loved so well.

D. started like an unbroke heifer when I interrupted him. A priori it was not very probable that

we should have met in Oriel. But D. would have
done the same, had I accosted him on the sudden
in his own walks in Clifford's Inn, or in the Temple.
In addition to a provoking short-sightedness (the
effect of late studies and watchings at the midnight
oil) D. is the most absent of men. He made a call
the other morning at our friend M.'s [Basil Mont-
agu's] in Bedford Square; and, finding nobody at
home, was ushered into the hall, where, asking for
pen and ink, with great exactitude of purpose he
enters his name in the book—which ordinarily lies
about in such places, to record the failures of the
untimely or unfortunate visitor—and takes his
leave with many ceremonies, and professions of
regret. Some two or three hours after, his walking
destinies returned him into the same neighbourhood
again, and again the quiet image of the fire-side
circle at M.'s—Mrs M. presiding at it like a Queen
Lar, with pretty A. S. [Ann Skipper, afterwards
Mrs B. W. Procter] at her side—striking irresistibly
on his fancy, he makes another call (forgetting that
they were "certainly not to return from the country
before that day week") and disappointed a second
time, enquires for pen and paper as before: again
the book is brought, and in the line just above that
in which he is about to print his second name (his
re-script)—his first name (scarce dry) looks out
upon him like another Sosid, or as if a man should
suddenly encounter his own duplicate! The effect
may be conceived. D. made many a good resolu-
tion against any such lapses in the future. I hope
he will not keep them too rigorously. For with
G. D.—to be absent from the body, is sometimes

(not to speak it profanely) to be present with the
Lord. At the very time when, personally en-
countering thee, he passes on with no recognition—
or being stopped, starts like a thing surprised—at
that moment, reader, he is on Mount Tabor—or
Parnassus—or co-sphered with Plato—or with
Harrington, framing "immortal commonwealths"
—devising some plan of amelioration to thy
country, or thy species—peradventure meditating
some individual kindness or courtesy, to be done
to *thee thyself*, the returning consciousness of which
made him to start so guiltily at thy obtruded per-
sonal presence....

It is neither upon his poetry nor his prose
but upon this passage and one other in Lamb's
Essays that George Dyer's title to fame reposes.
One other in particular; for the achievement of
his life, the deed by which he is known and
will be known throughout the ages, is his in-
voluntary dip in the New River in 1823. The
story is told in the Elia essay, "Amicus Redivivus." Lamb in writing a letter to Sarah
Hazlitt gives a more prosaic account of Dyer's
immersion in the New River. It is the first
draft of the Elia essay, "Amicus Redivivus,"
the best known, and most admired after the
"Dissertation upon Roast Pig." Lamb writes:

What I now tell you is literally true. Yesterday
week George Dyer called upon us, at one o'clock

[75]

(*bright noon day*) on his way to dine with Mrs
Barbauld at Newington. He sat with Mary about
half an hour, and took leave. The maid saw him go
out from her kitchen window, but suddenly losing
sight of him, ran up in a fright to Mary. G. D.,
instead of keeping the slip that leads to the gate,
had deliberately, staff in hand, in broad open day,
marched into the New River. He had not his
spectacles on, and you know his absence. Who
helped him out, they can hardly tell; but between
'em they got him out, drenched thro' and thro'.
A mob collected by that time and accompanied
him in. "Send for the Doctor!" they said: and a
one-eyed fellow, dirty and drunk, was fetched from
the Public House at the end, where it seems he
lurks, for the sake of picking up water practice,
having formerly had a medal from the Humane
Society for some rescue. By his advice, the patient
was put between blankets, and when I came home
at four to dinner, I found G. D. a-bed, and raving,
light-headed with the brandy-and-water which the
doctor had administered. He sung, laughed, whim-
pered, screamed, babbled of guardian angels, would
get up and go home; but we kept him there by force;
and by next morning he departed sobered, and seems
to have received no injury. All my friends are open-
mouthed about having paling before the river, but
I cannot see that, because a...lunatic chooses to
walk into a river with his eyes open at mid-day, I
am any the more likely to be drowned in it, coming
home at midnight.

There, in "Amicus Redivivus," we see Dyer

"vicariously making exquisite and imperishable literature."

Among other stories of Dyer's absence of mind is that told by Mrs Le Breton, in her *Memories of Seventy Years*, of his taking up a coal-scuttle in place of his hat; while on another occasion he walked off with a footman's cockaded hat, and did not discover his mistake until some one commiserated him on his fall in fortune. Talfourd's description of George Dyer mentions his "gaunt awkward form, set off by trousers too short...and a rusty coat as much too large for the wearer...his long head silvered over with short yet straggling hair, and his dark grey eyes." One or two of the inventions with which Lamb caused those eyes to glisten in faith and amazement are given in Talfourd's narrative, as when he told him in strict confidence that Castlereagh had confessed to the authorship of the Waverley Novels. Talfourd records also the perfect reply made by Dyer to Lamb's question, put to him to test his kindliness of heart, as to what he thought of the terrible Williams, the Ratcliffe Highway murderer (made immortal by De Quincey), who had first destroyed two families and then committed suicide. After a sufficient pause for consideration the answer came: "I should think, Mr

Lamb, he must have been rather an eccentric character." Dyer, poor enough in the early part of his life, was possessed of a sufficiency in his later years. The beginning of his good fortune was his inclusion among the two executors and residuary legatees of the third Lord Stanhope, "Citizen Stanhope," who died in 1816; George Dyer having at one time acted as tutor in his family.

It was probably just after Stanhope's death that Lamb, as Talfourd tells us, enquired gravely of Dyer if it were true, as commonly reported, that he was to be made a lord. "Oh dear no, Mr Lamb, I couldn't think of such a thing; it is not true, I assure you." "I thought not," said Lamb, "and I contradict it wherever I go; but the Government will not ask your consent, they may raise you to the Peerage without your ever knowing it." "I hope not, Mr Lamb, indeed, indeed, I hope not; it would not suit me at all." Leigh Hunt tells us that Dyer was one of the little trusting company whom Lamb sent to Primrose Hill to watch the Persian ambassador worshipping the sun. Though he made fun of Dyer's oddities, Lamb admired him and loved him always. "God never put a kinder heart into flesh of man than George Dyer's" he once said.

Although in Dyer's *Poetics* will be found a
sprightly and contented song on his persistent
celibacy, I imagine his singleness to have re-
sulted from the absence of temptation. As we
have seen, he had once loved; he had not
married, one suspects, simply because since
that time no woman had asked, or rather bidden,
him to do so. But somewhere about the year
1825 a widow "three deep," a Mrs Mather,
who had inherited from her third husband
chambers opposite Dyer's, was happily inspired
to suggest that he should accept her as wife and
guardian; and he did so with very pleasant
results, his only regret being expressed in a
remark once made to Crabb Robinson, "Mrs
Dyer is a woman of excellent natural sense, but
she is not literate." A charming account of the
marriage is given by Mrs Augustus De Morgan,
born Sophia Frend, a daughter of Dyer's coun-
sellor, William Frend of Cambridge. Mrs
Morgan writes, in her *Memoirs of Augustus De
Morgan*:

Late in life a tide came in his affairs. A kind
woman, the widow of a solicitor, who owned the
chambers opposite to his, watched him going in
and out, and saw his quiet harmless ways. As she
afterwards said in her Devonshire dialect, she
"couldn't abear to see the peure gentleman so
neglected." So she made acquaintance with him,

invited him across to the Inn, and gave him tea
and hot cakes and muffins "comfortable." At one
of these entertainments when the guest was expressing his satisfaction and thankfulness, she
observed: "Yes, Mr Dyer, sir, you *du* want some
one to look after you." The rejoinder was ready:
"Will you be that one." "Well, sir, I don't say
but what I've thought of it; but you must speak
to your friends, and let me see them, and if Mr
Frend approves...." So my father was informed
of the proposal, and in some alarm went to meet
the intended victim at the chambers of the "designing widow," who had already "buried" three
husbands. His views of the case were soon altered.
She was so simple, so open, and so evidently kind-
hearted, that, after examining and comparing all
circumstances, he thought that his old friend's
happiness would be secured by the marriage. It
took place shortly afterwards in St Dunstan's
Church in Fleet Street. When the newly married
pair came to visit us at Stoke Newington, we who
were in doubt as to what we were to expect were
pleased to find her a sensible, kindly-hearted
woman, who had made of our neglected old friend
a fine-looking, well-dressed elderly man, beaming
with kindness and happiness.

Another story of Dyer which Mrs De Morgan
tells illustrates Frend's sense of mischief as well
as the old scholar's mildness:

At one period of his life—I fancy before he went
as a sizar to Emmanuel College—Dyer was a
Baptist minister. I have seen his consternation and

[80]

alarm when thus reminded of his ministration by
my Father. Wm Frend: "You know, Dyer, that
was before you drowned the woman." G. Dyer:
"I never drowned any woman." Wm Frend: "You
have forgotten." To the company generally: "Dyer
had taken the woman's hand and made her dip in
the water; he then pronounced the blessing and
left her there." G. Dyer (troubled): "No, no; you
are joking. It could not be."

Cowden Clarke, writing of Dyer's marriage,
says:

It was great gratification to us to see how the
old student's rusty suit of black, threadbare and
shining with the shabbiness of neglect, the limp
wisp of Jaconet muslin, yellow with age, round his
throat, the dusty shoes, and stubbly beard, had
become exchanged for a coat that shone only with
the lustre of regular brushing, a snow-white cravat
neatly tied on, brightly blacked shoes, and a close-
shaven chin—the whole man presenting a cosy and
burnished appearance, like one carefully and affec-
tionately tended. He, like Charles Lamb, always
wore black smalls, black stockings (which Charles
Lamb generally covered with high black gaiters)
and black shoes; the knee smalls and the shoes
both being tied with strings instead of fastened
with buckles. His hair, white and stiff, glossy at
the time now spoken of from due administration
of comb and brush, contrasted strongly with a pair
of small dark eyes, worn with much poring over
Greek and black-letter characters; while even at
an advanced age there was a sweet look of kindli-

ness, simple goodness, serenity, and almost child-like guilelessness that characteristically marked his face at all periods of his life.

In Dyer's last years Crabb Robinson used to read to him occasionally on Sunday morning; but his customary help in this way came from a poor man who rendered his service for six-pence an hour. G. D. died on March 2nd, 1841, aged eighty-six all but a fortnight. William Frend was ill at the same time, dying on February 21st. The news of his death was kept from Dyer for some days, and Mrs De Morgan's beautiful account of George Dyer's last moments makes the end of the two friends synchronise:

During his last illness poor George Dyer sent up daily to enquire after him. When the messages came back for the last time, he asked for the news, and was told he was rather better. "I understand," he said, "Mr Frend is dead. Lay me beside him." He then went into the adjoining room, washed his hands, returned, and quietly sat down in his arm-chair, as it was thought to listen to a kind friend (Miss Mary Matilda Betham) who came to read to him. Before beginning she looked up at her hearer, but the loving-hearted old man was dead.

George Dyer's widow survived him for twenty years. She died in May, 1861, in her hundred and first year. Crabb Robinson called on her in August, 1860, when "she spoke in warm praise of Charles and Mary Lamb."

[82]

Ⅱ. "DYER'S FREND"

Friend of the friendless, friend of all mankind,
To thy wide friendships I have not been blind;
But looking at them nearly, in the end
I love thee most that thou art Dyer's Frend.

CHARLES LAMB.

THOUGH WILLIAM FREND is best known to
the world as "Dyer's Frend," as in Charles
Lamb's verse, yet his life is of interest especially
to Cambridge men. Before entering Christ's College as an undergraduate he had some unusual
experience. He was born in 1757, and educated
at Canterbury, was sent to St Omer to learn
French, and then to Quebec at the time of our
trouble with the Colonies. Frend was a patriot,
and there joined the Volunteers. As a student
at Christ's, in Paley's time, Frend read mathematics and took the degree of second wrangler.
He migrated to Jesus, took orders and became
Rector of St Michael's, Longstanton[1]. When
tutor of Jesus he turned Unitarian, and, for his
religious and political opinions, was expelled
the College, but not deprived of his Fellowship.
He published a tract entitled *Peace and Union
recommended to the associated bodies of Repub-
licans and Anti-Republicans,* for which he was

[1] Not of Madingley as in the *D.N.B.*

WILLIAM FREND

prosecuted in the Vice-Chancellor's court. This
was in the year 1793 at the time of the French
Revolution, "when civil dudgeon ran so high,
and men fell out they knew not why." Frend
was tried in the Senate House. "It appeared
from the first that the Vice-Chancellor was
determined to convict" him. Gunning, who
gives a detailed account of this trial, considers
that the prosecution was political rather than
religious. An interesting incident of Cambridge
undergraduate-life is recorded:

The undergraduates were unanimous in favour
of Mr Frend, and every satirical remark reflecting
on the conduct and motives of his prosecutors was
vociferously applauded. At length the court desired
the Proctors to interfere. Mr Farish, the Senior
Proctor, having marked one man who had particularly distinguished himself by applauding, and
noted his position in the Gallery of the Senate
House, selected him as a fit subject for punishment.
He went into the Gallery, and having previously
ascertained the exact position of the culprit, he
touched a person, whom he supposed to be the
same, on the shoulder, and asked him his name
and College. The person thus addressed assured
him that he had been perfectly quiet. Farish
replied: "I have been watching you for a long
time, and have seen you repeatedly clapping your
hands." "I wish this were possible," said the man,
and turning round exhibited an arm so deformed
that his hands could not by any possibility be

brought together; this exculpation was received
with repeated rounds of applause, which continued
for some minutes.

The name of the young man was Channock, and
his College Clare Hall; the real culprit was S. T.
Coleridge, of Jesus College, who having observed
that the Proctor had noticed him and was coming
into the gallery, turned round to the person who
was standing behind him and made an offer of
changing places, which was gladly accepted by
the unsuspecting man. Coleridge immediately
retreated, and mixing with the crowd, entirely
escaped suspicion. This conduct on the part of
Coleridge was severely censured by the undergraduates, as it was quite clear that, to escape
punishment himself, he would have subjected an
innocent man to rustication or expulsion.

Coleridge was an excellent classical scholar; he
affected a peculiar style in conversation and his
language was very poetical. An instance has at
this moment occurred to me. Speaking of the
dinners in Hall, he described the veal which was
served up to them (and which was large and coarse)
in the following words: "We have veal, sir, tottering
on the verge of beef!" The topic on which Coleridge
much delighted to converse was the establishment
of a society consisting of twelve members, each of
whom, after having learned some handicraft (I
think he was learning to be a carpenter) should
select a highly-accomplished woman, who should
accompany them to some remote and uninhabited
country, where they should form a colony of themselves. He and Southey married two sisters, whom

they first saw at Bristol. The projected colonisation never took place; but a button-manufacturer at Birmingham (who was to have been one of the party) defrayed all the expenses that had been incurred to carry out this wild scheme.

Frend, though driven from his College and University, was known as a scholar, and astonished his friends by refusing to go as tutor to the Archduke Alexander with a salary of £2000 a year, and a pension. He went to London and became actuary to the Rock Life Insurance Company with a residence and a handsome salary. He married a granddaughter of Archdeacon Blackburn, whose portrait is in St Catharine's College.

Frend wrote a great deal, besides his mathematical works. He was a good Hebrew scholar and had wide political and social knowledge. He wrote papers on "Scarcity of Bread," "Principles of Taxation," "Baptism," "The National Debt," "The Slave Trade" and "Patriotism."

In 1838, when Frend was four score years of age, he wrote a letter to Lady Byron containing the following reminiscence:

Every prejudice removed makes way for the progress of truth. I look back fifty years, and if I had then said I should live to see a Papist one year, and two years following two Jews should be

Sheriffs of London, I should have been laughed at; and if I had added, being then in the University, that a Quaker should become one year Fourth Wrangler, and in another year a Jew Second Wrangler, the laughter of the gods would have been less than that of my hearers.

Many of William Frend's descendants were distinguished in learning, arts and literature; besides the barrister already mentioned, the De Morgans were notable people. Augustus De Morgan, the mathematician, married Sophia Elizabeth, the daughter of William Frend, and their son, William Frend De Morgan, was the well-known potter and novelist who gave us *Joseph Vance* and *Alice-for-short*.

A pedigree before me, which is too long to publish, would satisfy the learned author of *Hereditary Genius*. It includes Miss Constance Phillott, the artist, and Miss Frances Phillott Seeley, the daughter of the Cambridge Professor, Sir John Seeley. William Frend lies buried in Kensal Green with George Dyer beside him.

[87]

INDEX OF DINERS

THE following is a record of those who attended the Charles Lamb Dinners at Cambridge, 1909–14:

Chairmen

1909 GEORGE WHERRY, M.A.
1910 [The late] H. M. BUTLER, D.D.
1911 [The late] HENRY JACKSON, O.M.

1912 [Sir] F. DARWIN, SC.D.
1913 [Sir] A. E. SHIPLEY, SC.D.
1914 [The late Rt Hon. Sir] T. CLIFFORD ALLBUTT, K.C.B.

Guests

1909 RT HON. A. BIRRELL.
1910 E. V. LUCAS.
1911 [The late Sir] W. A. RALEIGH, M.A.

1912 [Sir] EDMUND GOSSE.
1913 [Sir] HENRY NEW-BOLT.
1914 G. S. STREET.

Diners

ABRAHAMS, I. (1913, 1914)
ALFORD, J. (1912)
ALLBUTT, PROF. [SIR] T. CLIFFORD (1909–11, 1914)
APPLETON, RICHARD (1909)
ARMITAGE, C. A. (1910, 1911)
ASTON, W. D. (1910)

BAINBRIGGE, P. G. (1912)

BALL, W. W. ROUSE (1911)
BARBER, W. E. (1913)
BARNETT, B. L. (1914)
BARTHOLOMEW, A. T. (1909–14)
BATHURST, HON. L. (1913)
BAYFIELD, M. A. (1909)
BEAUMONT, REV. W. E. (1909)
BECK, E. (1910)
BENHAM, B. (1914)

BENIANS, E. A. (1910, 1913)
BENNETT, J. R. STERNDALE (1910)
BENSON, DR A. C. (1910)
BERNAYS, A. E. (1910–14)
BIRCH, F. L. (1913)
BIRRELL, F. F. L. (1909, 1910)
BLACKMAN, F. F. (1912)
BLANDFORD, F. G. (1910)
BRINDLEY, H. H. (1910–13)
BROOKE, RUPERT (1909, 1913)
BROWN, B. GOULDING (1910–14)
BULLOUGH, E. (1910, 1911)
BURTON, H. P. W. (1911)
BUTLER, DR H. M. (1910)

CAMPBELL, A. Y. (1913)
CHARRINGTON, J. (1910)
CLARKE, F. W. (1911)
COTTON, V. E. (1909)
COULTON, G. G. (1913)

DAHLGREN, PROF. E. W. (1913)
DALTON, H. (1910)
DARWIN, [SIR] F. (1910–13)
DARWIN, H. (1913)
DAVIES, R. (1909)
DENT, E. J. (1914)
DENT, J. M. (1909, 1911)
DON, A. W. R. (1911, 1912)
DONALDSON, DR S. A. (1911, 1912)
DOWNS, B. W. (1914)
DUFF, J. D. (1911)
DURNFORD, [SIR] W. (1910)

EDWARDS, H. J. (1911)
ELLIOT, H. (1912)
ELLIS, W. F. P. (1912)
EVANS, H. S. (1910)

FLETCHER, S. S. F. (1910)
FLETCHER, [SIR] W. M. (1911–13)
FORBES, M. D. (1912–14)
FRY, G. S. (1909, 1911)

GARRETT, H. F. (1910, 1911)
GIBB, E. A. (1912)
GIBBS, C. A. (1910, 1911)
GILES, CAPT. (1914)
GILES, PROF. H. A. (1909–14)
GORDON, C. (1909)
GRAY, DR ALAN (1911, 1913)
GRAY, BASIL (1910)
GRAY, M. (1913)
GREAVES, J. (1910, 1911, 1913)
GREEN, A. J. B. (1910)
GREEN, J. R. (1909)
GREENE, F. C. (1910–13)
GREIG, A. F. M. (1912)
GROSE, S. W. (1909)
GUILLEMARD, DR F. H. H. (1909, 1910, 1912)

HARDMAN, F. M. (1913)
HARDY, [SIR] W. B. (1911)
HASLAM, W. H. (1911)
HAWARD, L. W. (1914)
HENRY, A. (1911–13)
HOPE, J. H. (1914)
HOPKINS, [PROF. SIR] F. G. (1910, 1911, 1913)

HUGHES, G. R. (1914)
HUTCHINSON, F. E. (1909)
JACKSON, DR HENRY (1910, 1911, 1913, 1914)
JACKSON, [SIR] H. (1909–11)
JONES, E. A. (1913)

KEYNES, J. M. (1909–12)
KNAPPETT, P. G. (1909)
KNOX, A. D. (1913)

LAMB, W. R. M. (1911–13)
LANE, JOHN (1913)
LANG, H. (1912)
LAYARD, J. W. (1914)
LONGWORTH, E. C. (1911)
LUMBY, C. D. R. (1909)

MACAULAY, G. C. (1910–12)
MACKAY, R. F. B. (1913)
MALLORY, G. H. L. (1909)
MALLORY, G. T. (1912)
MARCHAND, G. (1911, 1912)
MARSH, E. (1913)
MARSH, DR F. HOWARD (1909–14)
MᶜLEAN, N. (1910)
MIDDLEMAS, P. (1913)
MOREL, J. (1912)
MOULE, C. W. (1910–12)

NIXON, F. H. (1911–14)
NOBLE, H. B. (1913, 1914)
NON, A. (1913)
NUTTALL, PROF. G. H. F. (1910)

OATFIELD, W. J. (1913)

PARRY, A. H. (1914)
PARRY, DR R. ST J. (1909, 1911–13)
PARTRIDGE, G. J. (1913)
PICCOLI, R. (1914)
PLIMMER, H. G. (1912)
POPHAM, A. E. (1911)
POTTS, F. A. (1913)
PRACY, H. E. F. (1914)
PURVES, C. L. (1911)

RAMSAY, A. (1910–12)
RAPSON, PROF. E. J. (1909–14)
RAVERAT, J. P. (1913)
RENDALL, V. (1911)
RICHMOND, O. L. (1912, 1913)
ROBERTS, S. C. (1912–14)
ROBERTSON, D. H. (1909)
ROBINSON, F. P. (1910, 1914)
ROTH, G. J. (1912, 1913)
ROUQUETTE, D. (1913)
ROUSE, DR W. H. D. (1910–13)
ROUTH, H. V. (1913, 1914)
RUSSELL SMITH, H. F. (1910, 1913)

SALTER, F. R. (1911, 1912)
SANDFORD, G. R. (1912)
SAYLE, C. (1909–14)
SCALES, F. S. (1911, 1912)
SEWARD, PROF. A. C. (1909–14)
SHAW, C. G. (1911)
SHEPPARD, J. T. (1909, 1911)

[90]

SHIPLEY, [SIR] A. E. (1911, 1913)
SHOVE, G. F. (1910, 1911)
SPRING RICE, E. D. (1910)
SQUIRE, J. C. (1912, 1914)
STEWART, DR H. F. (1909, 1911–13)
STOKES, DR H. P. (1909–14)
STORRS, C. (1909, 1910)
STRACHEY, J. (1911)

TAYLOR, C. F. (1911)
TAYLOR, SEDLEY (1914)
THOMPSON, F. W. (1909, 1911)
TOULMIN, G. E. (1911, 1914)
TOYE, F. (1914)
TREND, J. B. (1911, 1912)
TURNER, A. C. (1910)

VALE, E. (1912)
VON [DE] GLEHN, L. (1910)

WARDALE, J. R. (1911, 1912)
WARDLEY, G. C. N. (1912, 1914)
WEBSTER, C. K. (1913)
WHERRY, GEORGE (1909–14)
WILLIAMS, I. A. (1911–14)
WILSON, J. S. (1909)
WOOD, H. G. (1910)
WRIGHT, H. (1909–13)
WYATT, A. J. (1911)

YEATMAN, F. D. (1911–13)
YOUNG, G. W. (1909–13)

CAMBRIDGE: *printed by* W. LEWIS *at the University Press*

Lightning Source UK Ltd.
Milton Keynes UK
UKHW010747060819
347479UK00001B/23/P